Picnics

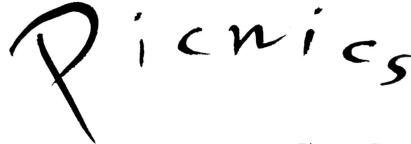

Picnics

Elegant Recipes for
Alfresco Dining

Barbara Scott-Goodman

Illustrations by
Maxine Boll-Hughes

CHRONICLE BOOKS
SAN FRANCISCO

For Lester, Zan, and Isabelle

I'd like to thank all of my family, friends, and associates:
Bill LeBlond, Leslie Jonath, Sarah Putman, Anne Galperin, and all of the talented people
at Chronicle Books.
Maxine Boll-Hughes for her beautiful watercolors.
David Grotenstein, cheese maven, for his knowledge and his generosity with it.
Bob Cornfield, my agent, advisor, and friend.
Lester, my husband and partner, and Zan and Isabelle, my kids,
who always bring out the best in me.

Library of Congress Cataloging-in-Publication Data:
Scott-Goodman, Barbara.
Picnics: elegant recipes for alfresco dining/Barbara Scott-Goodman.
p. cm.
Includes index.
ISBN 0-8118-2078-5 (HC)
1. Picnicking. 2. Outdoor cookery. I. Title.
TX823.S37 1999
641.5'78—dc21   98-30314
CIP

Printed in Singapore.

Distributed in Canada by Raincoast Books
8680 Cambie Street
Vancouver, British Columbia V6P 6M9

10 9 8 7 6 5 4 3 2 1

Chronicle Books
85 Second Street
San Francisco, California 94105

www.chroniclebooks.com

Table of Contents

Introduction

Whether it's an elaborate gathering with picnic hampers filled with all of the makings of a formal picnic lunch—good china, linen napkins, and champagne flutes—or a simple lunch of sandwiches and fresh lemonade eaten on the back porch, just the idea of eating outside in beautiful weather makes me happy. I love picnics and have them as often as possible.

One of the virtues of a picnic is its flexibility. A picnic can be held almost anywhere: at the beach in the late afternoon, in the woods during a hike, on a boat at the lake, on the roadside while traveling with the family, in the park before a concert. Closer to home, a picnic can be casual, under a tree in the backyard, or on the deck or patio, or it can be formal, such as an alfresco dinner on the terrace with candlelight.

The recipes in this book are suited to all types of picnics. For a beach barbecue, try Grilled Chicken Kebabs with Peach Salsa; Orzo, Salmon, Corn, and Chive Salad; and Perfect Picnic Brownies. Or you may like Deviled Eggs, Country-Style Buttermilk Biscuits, Tarragon-Rosemary Roasted Chicken, salad, and Chilled

Minted Fruit for a down-home spread under the trees in your backyard. For an elaborate picnic, you may want to serve Chilled Carrot, Orange, and Chive Soup; Tomato and Dill Sandwiches with Smoked Salmon–Caper Spread; New Potato, Green Bean, and Dill Salad; followed by Cinnamon-Peach Cake. Your guests will clamor for more.

A picnic doesn't have to be labor intensive. For an impromptu, take-out picnic, pick up some of the makings—a selection of cheeses, salamis and sausages, pâtés, olives, and a few loaves of bread—at your local market or favorite deli and round out the menu with the fare you prepare from this book. Buy some cherry tomatoes, cucumbers, and radishes at the produce market and a freshly made dessert at the bakery if you're short on time. Pack your cooler with sweet butter, a few mustards, salt and pepper, wine, and beer (don't forget the knives and the corkscrew!) and enjoy the pleasures of outdoor dining.

Although picnics are not complicated meals that involve careful timing or a great deal of your attention at the stove just before serving, great picnics do need to be well planned. Once you have your location and date set, your menu planned, and your picnic hamper ready, go out and enjoy one of life's greatest pleasures—the picnic.

Small Bites

DEVILED EGGS

*W*hat is a picnic without deviled eggs? They are so tasty and there are so many ways to make them. Deviled eggs can be simply prepared with chopped herbs and vegetables and a myriad of spices, or they can be elegantly dressed up with smoked salmon or caviar. This is my basic deviled egg recipe.

---

6 large eggs
¼ cup finely chopped flat-leaf
   parsley
½ cup mayonnaise
1 tablespoon Dijon mustard
Salt and freshly ground black pepper,
   to taste
Parsley sprigs, for garnish

---

1. Put the eggs in a large pot and cover with cold water. Bring to a gentle boil. When the water just begins to boil, turn off the heat and cover the pot tightly. Let the eggs stand, covered, for 30 minutes. Drain the eggs and rinse them in cold water. Pat the eggs dry and let cool.

2. When the eggs are cool enough to handle, peel them and slice them lengthwise. Scoop the yolks out and put them in a large mixing bowl. Set the egg whites aside on a platter.

3. Mash the yolks with a fork, and add the chopped parsley. Stir in the mayonnaise and mustard and mix well. Add the salt and pepper to taste.

4. Spoon the egg yolk mixture into the egg white halves. Top with parsley sprigs, if desired. The deviled eggs may be refrigerated for up to 3 hours before serving.

Deviled Egg Variations

There are a number of ways to create delicious variations of the basic deviled egg recipe. Add any of the following combinations to the hard-boiled egg yolks before mixing with mayonnaise and mustard.

◆ Add ½ cup sour cream instead of mayonnaise,
2 tablespoons chopped black olives, and a pinch of paprika.

◆ Add ¼ cup each finely chopped anchovies and celery.

◆ Add ¼ cup finely chopped crabmeat and fresh lemon juice to taste.

◆ Add 2 tablespoons each finely chopped pecans and chives.

◆ Add 2 tablespoons each finely chopped red pepper and
cilantro and ½ teaspoon ground cumin.

◆ Add 2 tablespoons each finely chopped yellow peppers
and scallions and a pinch of cayenne pepper.

◆ Add 2 tablespoons each finely chopped red onions and capers.

◆ Add 2 tablespoons each finely chopped ham and watercress.

◆ Add ¼ cup finely chopped smoked salmon, 2 tablespoons finely
minced dill, and lemon juice to taste. Garnish with dill sprigs.

◆ Add 2 tablespoons of caviar. Garnish with a dollop of
crème fraîche and additional caviar.

Marinated Mushrooms

Serves 8, makes 4 dozen mushrooms

*T*hese aromatic mushrooms make a wonderful summer hors d'oeuvre. They can be made well ahead of time and stored in the refrigerator for up to one week.

¾ cup olive oil
½ cup water
¼ cup red wine vinegar
Juice of 1 lemon
1 tablespoon dry sherry
3 cloves garlic
2 tablespoons ground coriander
   seeds
1 tablespoon herbes de Provence
2 teaspoons fennel seeds
½ teaspoon dried thyme
2 bay leaves
Salt and freshly ground black
   pepper, to taste
1½ pounds (about 4 dozen) small
   white mushrooms, rinsed and
   patted dry

1. Mix together the oil, water, vinegar, lemon juice, sherry, garlic, coriander, herbes de Provence, fennel seeds, thyme, bay leaves, and salt and pepper in a large stockpot. Bring the

mixture to a boil over medium-high heat, and then reduce the heat and simmer for 10 minutes.

2. Add the mushrooms to the pot, stirring to coat them with sauce.

3. Remove the pot from the heat and let the mushrooms cool to room temperature in the pot, about 1 hour.

4. Using a slotted spoon, remove the mushrooms to a serving dish. Pour the cooking liquid over the mushrooms. Refrigerate for at least 2 hours or overnight. *Note: they will keep in the refrigerator for at least a week.*

5. Serve chilled or at room temperature with toothpicks.

`` ` ` ` ` ` ` ` ` ` ` ` ``

A Summertime Feast in the Country

◆

Marinated Mushrooms

◆

Deviled Eggs

◆

Tarragon-Rosemary Roasted Chicken

Jicama, Orange, Watercress, and Pecan Salad

Country-Style Buttermilk Biscuits

◆

Chilled Minted Fruit

◆

*chilled white wine
iced tea*

SPICY BLACK BEAN DIP

Serves 8 to 10, makes 1½ cups

*T*his rich and spicy dip is wonderful with blue corn tortilla chips. It is best to make it a day or two ahead of time to allow the flavors to intensify.

½ pound black beans, rinsed and
   picked over
1 medium onion, coarsely chopped
2 carrots, peeled and chopped
1 tomato, peeled, seeded, and
   chopped
2 cloves garlic, thinly sliced
2 jalapeño chile peppers, seeded
   and minced
2 teaspoons ground cumin
Salt and freshly ground black pepper,
   to taste
½ cup hot chicken stock, preferably
   homemade
1 tablespoon chile powder
¼ cup chopped fresh cilantro

---

1. Put the beans in a large bowl, cover by about 2 inches with cold water, and soak for 6 to 8 hours or overnight.

2. Drain the beans and place them in a large stockpot with the onion, carrots, one-half of the chopped tomato, garlic, peppers, 1 teaspoon of the cumin, and salt and pepper. Cover with water, bring to a boil, and simmer over medium-low heat until the beans are very tender, about 1 hour. Add more water during cooking, if necessary.

3. Drain and set the bean mixture aside. When cool enough to handle, blend the mixture in a food processor fitted with a steel blade. Add enough of the stock to make a smooth purée. Add the remaining chopped tomato and cumin, chili powder, and cilantro and purée again until smooth. Taste and adjust the seasonings, if necessary.

4. Refrigerate for at least 24 hours before serving.

HERBED GREEN BEANS WITH
MOZZARELLA AND PROSCIUTTO

Serves 6 to 8

*T*his is one of the prettiest and easiest finger foods to make. Fresh green beans are wrapped in paper-thin slices of mozzarella and prosciutto, then drizzled with an herb vinaigrette.

---

2 pounds green beans, trimmed and cut into 3-inch lengths
½ pound prosciutto or Parma ham, thinly sliced
1 pound fresh mozzarella, thinly sliced
¼ cup red wine vinegar
½ cup extra-virgin olive oil
2 tablespoons chopped fresh basil
2 tablespoons chopped fresh dill
Salt and freshly ground black pepper, to taste

---

1. Cook the beans in enough boiling salted water to cover for about 3 minutes, or until crisp-tender. Drain and rinse under cold running water. Drain again.

2. Place a slice of prosciutto on a plate and top with a slice of the mozzarella. Place about 6 beans in the center of the cheese and fold both the sides over to encase the beans. Arrange the wraps on a platter.

3. In a small bowl, whisk the vinegar and oil until thickened. Add the basil, dill, and the salt and pepper and whisk again. Drizzle the vinaigrette over the green bean wraps.

4. Refrigerate for at least 1 hour before serving.

Lemon-Fennel Olives

Makes two 1-pint jars

*T*his preparation is a great way to enhance any type of olive. Choose from a variety of types of olives. The olives are layered with fennel and lemon slices, and fruity olive oil is poured over them. It's just the thing for a special picnic, and it can be made up to a month ahead of time.

1½ pounds olives, drained and rinsed
1 lemon, thinly sliced
½ bulb fennel, trimmed and thinly sliced lengthwise
4 cloves garlic, thinly sliced
1 tablespoon black peppercorns
1 tablespoon fennel seeds
Extra-virgin olive oil, to cover

---

1. Put a layer of olives in the bottom of a 1-pint glass jar. Add several slices of the lemon, fennel and garlic, and sprinkle with some of the peppercorns and fennel seeds. Continue layering until the jar is full. Cover the olives with olive oil and seal the jar tightly.

Repeat this process with the second 1-pint jar.

2. Refrigerate the olives for 24 hours before serving. They may be stored in the refrigerator for up to 1 month. Bring to room temperature before serving.

Olives

There are dozens of varieties of olives which differ in size, color, and flavor. Use any combination of them when making Lemon-Fennel Olives. Here are some suggestions.

◆ Gaeta (Italian): Black or brown, small, and wrinkled.

◆ Kalamata (Greek): Purple-black, almond-shaped, and shiny. They are available in a variety of sizes.

◆ Ligurian (Italian): Black or brown. The black ones are very flavorful.

◆ Niçoise (French): Very small and dark brown or black, with a large pit.

◆ Nyons (French): Small and well known for their reddish-brown color.

◆ Picholine (French): Small and medium green in color.

Soups,
Sandwiches,
and
Savories

YELLOW-PEPPER GAZPACHO

Serves 6

*G*azpacho is a refreshing cold soup. This robust and colorful version, full of fresh yellow peppers, cucumbers, red onions, and ripe tomatoes, is topped with thinly sliced avocado.

---

4 medium yellow bell peppers, seeded, deveined, and finely chopped

2 medium cucumbers, peeled, seeded, and coarsely chopped

1 medium red onion, peeled and coarsely chopped

2 cloves garlic, thinly sliced

4 large ripe tomatoes, cored and cut into wedges

2 cups chicken stock, preferably homemade

⅓ cup balsamic vinegar

2 tablespoons capers, drained

Salt and freshly ground black pepper, to taste

1 ripe avocado, peeled, pitted, and thinly sliced, for garnish

---

1. Place all of the ingredients except the avocado in a large bowl and stir to mix well.

2. Purée half of the mixture in a blender or food processor fitted with a steel blade. This may have to be done in batches.

3. Return the purée to the bowl and mix well. Taste and adjust seasoning, if necessary. Cover and refrigerate for at least 4 hours.

4. To serve, stir, ladle into chilled soup mugs, and top each serving with avocado slices.

CHILLED CARROT, ORANGE, AND CHIVE SOUP

Serves 6

*G*arnished with a dollop of yogurt, this cool soup is a perfect picnic starter. It soothes and refreshes the palate on a summer afternoon.

---

4 tablespoons unsalted butter

2 medium white onions, peeled and chopped

12 large carrots, peeled and diced

4 cups chicken stock, preferably homemade

1 cup water

½ cup fresh orange juice

Pinch of cayenne pepper

¼ cup minced chives

Salt and freshly ground black pepper, to taste

Plain yogurt, for garnish

---

1. Melt the butter in a stockpot over low heat. Add the onions, cover, and cook until tender, about 20 minutes.

2. Add the carrots, stock, and water. Bring to a boil, reduce the heat, and simmer, partially covered, for about 20 minutes, until the carrots are tender. Remove the pot from the heat and let the soup cool for about 1 hour.

3. Purée the soup in batches in a blender or a food processor fitted with a steel blade. Return the purée to the pot and add the orange juice, cayenne, chives, and salt and pepper to taste. Cover and refrigerate for at least 4 hours.

4. To serve, stir, ladle into chilled soup mugs, and top each serving with a dollop of yogurt.

CHILLED CREAMY CLAM CHOWDER

Serves 6

Served with baguettes and a chilled white wine, this elegant version of clam chowder is a meal in itself.

---

4 slices bacon, cut into ½-inch dice

2 tablespoons unsalted butter

1 large white onion, peeled and
chopped

1 cup bottled clam juice

1½ cups dry white wine

2 cups water

3 russet potatoes, peeled and cut
into ½-inch dice

18 littleneck clams, shelled, chopped,
and drained, juice reserved

½ teaspoon dried thyme

Dash of Tabasco sauce

1 cup milk

1 cup heavy whipping cream

Salt and freshly ground black pepper,
to taste

2 tablespoons dry sherry

Finely chopped fresh dill, for garnish

Finely chopped fresh parsley,
for garnish

---

1. Fry the bacon in a large stockpot over medium-high heat, until crisp. Using a slotted spoon, transfer the bacon to paper towels to drain. Save the bacon for another use or discard. Pour out and discard all but 1 table-spoon of bacon fat.

2. Add the butter to the bacon fat in the stockpot and heat over low heat. Add the onion and cook for 10 min-utes, stirring occasionally, until tender. Add the clam juice, wine, water, and potatoes. Bring to a boil and then reduce the heat and simmer until the potatoes are just tender, about 25 minutes.

3. Add the clams and their juice, thyme, and Tabasco sauce and sim-mer for 5 minutes longer. Stir in the milk, cream, and salt and pepper to taste. When the soup is just barely

boiling, stir in the sherry. Remove the pot from the heat and let the soup cool for about 1 hour.

4. Purée the soup in batches in a blender or a food processor fitted with a steel blade. Return the purée to the pot and taste and adjust seasoning, if necessary. Cover and refrigerate for at least 3 hours.

5. To serve, stir, ladle into chilled soup mugs, and garnish with a sprinkling of chopped dill and parsley.

GRILLED LAMB, ROASTED EGGPLANT, RED PEPPER, AND ONION SANDWICHES

Makes 12 sandwiches

This sensational sandwich is made with grilled butterflied leg of lamb and savory roasted vegetables. Everything can be prepared ahead of time and then assembled on baguettes. The sandwiches can then be drizzled with olive oil or spread with mayonnaise or mustard, depending on your guests' tastes, and packed in your picnic basket.

LAMB:

½ cup red wine vinegar

1 teaspoon herbes de Provence

4 large cloves garlic, thinly sliced

2 tablespoons low-sodium soy sauce

Freshly ground black pepper

⅓ cup olive oil

One 3- to 4-pound butterflied leg of lamb

VEGETABLES:

1 medium eggplant (about 1 pound), peeled and cut into ½-inch slices

3 medium red bell peppers, seeded and halved

3 medium red onions, peeled and cut into ¼-inch-thick slices

2 tablespoons kosher salt

1 tablespoon dried rosemary

7 tablespoons olive oil

Six 8-inch baguettes or hero rolls, halved lengthwise

Olive oil, Dijon mustard or mayonnaise, optional

---

1. To prepare the lamb: Stir the vinegar, herbes de Provence, garlic, soy sauce, and pepper together in a medium bowl. Whisk in the olive oil. Place the lamb in a large, shallow glass or ceramic baking dish. Pour the marinade over the lamb, cover, and refrigerate for about 6 hours, turning the lamb occasionally.

2. Prepare a charcoal or gas grill until the coals are covered with white ash.

3. Remove the lamb from the marinade, reserving the marinade. Grill the lamb 4 to 6 inches from the coals for about 40 minutes, basting frequently with the marinade and turning it at least once. Check the lamb for doneness after 30 minutes; do not overcook. Set aside to cool for about 15 minutes, then carve the lamb into thin slices.

4. To prepare the vegetables: preheat the oven to 375°F.

5. Place the eggplant slices on an aluminum foil–lined baking sheet. Place the red peppers and onions on a separate foil-lined baking sheet.

Sprinkle with the kosher salt and rosemary. Pour 4 tablespoons of the olive oil over the eggplant. Pour the remaining 3 tablespoons olive oil over the peppers and onions, and place the two pans in the oven. Roast the eggplant until lightly browned and tender, about 35 minutes. Remove the eggplant from the oven and set aside to cool. Continue to roast the peppers and onions until browned and softened, about 1 hour. Remove the peppers and onions from the oven and set aside to cool.

6. To assemble the sandwiches: Lay several slices of lamb on 6 of the baguette or roll halves and top with the eggplant, red pepper, and onions. Drizzle olive oil, or spread mustard or mayonnaise over the vegetables, if desired. Place the tops of the baguettes over the vegetables and slice the sandwiches crosswise.

TOMATO AND DILL SANDWICHES WITH
SMOKED SALMON–CAPER SPREAD

Makes 6 full-sized sandwiches or 18 tea sandwiches

This delectable smoked salmon–caper spread is fabulous on slices of rye or pumpernickel bread, and it can be prepared several hours ahead of time. For a more elegant picnic, slice into little tea sandwiches.

Two 8-ounce packages cream cheese,
*   at room temperature*
½ cup chopped fresh parsley
4 tablespoons fresh lemon juice
2 tablespoons heavy whipping cream
2 tablespoons capers, drained
½ pound smoked salmon
12 slices pumpernickel or rye bread
2 large ripe tomatoes, thinly sliced
Dill sprigs

---

1. Put the cream cheese, parsley, lemon juice, heavy cream, capers, and 6 ounces of the salmon in the bowl of a food processor fitted with the steel blade and process until smooth, stopping the machine once during processing to scrape down the sides of the work bowl. Add the remaining salmon and mix briefly until just incorporated. Cover and refrigerate.

2. To assemble the sandwiches, generously spread 6 slices of the bread with the smoked salmon mixture. Top with tomato slices and dill sprigs and slice in half. If you are making tea sandwiches, instead of cutting the sandwiches in half, cut them into 1½-by-3-inch rectangles.

GRILLED STEAK AND ROASTED
RED ONION RING SANDWICHES

Makes 6 sandwiches

This wonderful, hearty sandwich is great for a picnic lunch, perhaps following an active morning of swimming, hiking, or bicycling. These sandwiches taste especially good served with a side of Red Cabbage, Pepper, and Onion Coleslaw (page 36) and ice-cold beer.

MARINATED STEAK:

½ cup red wine vinegar
¼ cup low-sodium soy sauce
¼ cup olive oil
2½ pounds sirloin, 1-inch-thick,
   (top round or flank steak)

ONION RINGS:

4 medium red onions, peeled and
   cut into ¼-inch-thick rings
2 tablespoons olive oil
Salt and freshly ground black pepper,
   to taste

12 slices pumpernickel or rye bread
Mayonnaise or mustard
Boston or Bibb lettuce, coarsely
   shredded

1. Combine the vinegar and soy sauce in a small bowl. Whisk in the olive oil. Place the steak in a large glass or ceramic baking dish and pour the marinade over it. Cover and refrigerate for up to 3 hours, or overnight. Turn the steak occasionally.

2. Prepare a gas or charcoal grill.

3. Grill the steak over medium-hot coals for 4 to 5 minutes to a side for rare meat and 6 to 7 minutes for medium. Baste with the marinade several times during grilling. Remove the steak to a cutting board and carve on the diagonal into ⅜-inch-thick slices. Cover the meat with plastic wrap and refrigerate to chill.

4. To prepare the onion rings, preheat the oven to 350°F. Place the sliced onions in a roasting pan. Toss with the 2 tablespoons olive oil and salt and pepper. Roast the onions until fork-tender, about 1 hour.

5. To assemble the sandwiches, generously spread the bread with the mayonnaise or mustard. Divide the sliced steak between 6 of the bread slices and cover it with the roasted onion rings. Top with the shredded lettuce and the remaining bread and cut the sandwiches in half.

Lunch on the Patio

◆

*Chilled Carrot, Orange,
and Chive Soup*

◆

*Grilled Steak and
Roasted Red Onion Ring
Sandwiches*

*New Potato, Green Bean,
and Dill Salad*

*Red Cabbage, Pepper,
and Onion Coleslaw*

◆

*Lemon Wafers
sorbet*

◆

*chilled rosé
lemonade*

Red Pepper, Scallion, and Mint Frittata

Serves 6

*F*rittatas are excellent picnic fare. They are light yet substantial, and they are versatile, too. They can be cut into squares or wedges for easy eating and they can be served warm, cold, or at room temperature. Mint, that ubiquitous summer herb, offers a deliciously unusual flavor.

---

1 tablespoon unsalted butter

1 tablespoon olive oil

2 tablespoons minced yellow onion

1 medium red bell pepper, seeded, deveined, and cut into ½-inch dice

6 scallions, trimmed and minced

5 large eggs, at room temperature

4 tablespoons finely chopped fresh mint leaves

½ cup half-and-half

Salt and freshly ground black pepper, to taste

2½ ounces Gruyère cheese, cut into ½-inch cubes (about ½ cup)

3 tablespoons freshly grated Parmesan cheese

---

1. Preheat the oven to 350°F.

2. Heat the butter and oil together in a large skillet over medium-high heat until the foam begins to subside. Add the onion and red pepper and cook until tender, about 10 minutes. Stir in the scallions and cook until just tender, about 2 minutes. Remove from the heat.

3. Butter a 10-inch round or an 11¾-by-7½-inch rectangular glass or ceramic baking dish. Spread the onion mixture in the dish.

4. In a large mixing bowl, combine the eggs, mint, half-and-half, and salt and pepper. Pour the mixture into the baking dish and dot with the cubed cheese; press the cheese pieces

slightly into the egg mixture, sprinkle with the Parmesan, and bake until the top is lightly browned, 35 to 40 minutes. Remove from the oven and let cool slightly.

5. Serve the frittata warm or at room temperature, or refrigerate the frittata and serve cold.

Cheeses

*I*f the mood strikes to have a picnic but you don't have time to cook, you can create a wonderful impromptu feast by choosing a selection of cheeses, pâtés, sausages, bread, fruit, and wine to pack in your cooler. Or instead of baking, serve cheese and fruit for a delightful picnic dessert. Here are some tips on cheese.

When buying cheese for a picnic, think in terms of taste, texture, and contrast. Choose at least two or three cheeses from different categories. Because your leftover cheese will not keep well, plan on bringing only the amount of cheese you plan to serve. A good rule of thumb is about two to three ounces per person.

Cheese should be well wrapped when packing it. Wrap cheeses in plastic wrap or wax paper and dab off any moisture that may have accumulated on them. Also, be sure to store your cooler in a shady place, not in the sun. Here is a sampling of a few good cheeses to take on a picnic.

Hard Cheeses

◆ *Asiago:* Look for the excellent Italian-inspired Stella Asiago from Wisconsin. It is made from part-skim cow's milk. This cheese has a rich, nutty flavor and is good with peasant bread and black olives.

◆ *Cheddar:* There are a number of good Cheddars to choose from. Among them are Somerset Farmhouse Cheddar from England; Black Diamond Cheddar from Canada; Cabot's Private Stock, Grafton Village, and Shelbourne Farms from Vermont; and Tillamook Cheddar from Oregon. Cheddar cheese is delicious with apples and grapes. Drink a full-bodied wine such as Cabernet Sauvignon or dark beer or cider with this cheese.

◆ *Dry Jack:* This is a Monterey Jack cheese that is aged 6 months to 2 years. Look for Bear Flag Brand from Sonoma, California. Dry Jack is reminiscent of Parmesan but is less grainy. It is very good with apples and ripe plums.

◆ *Parmigiano-Reggiano:* This king of Italian cheeses has a wonderful, rich, nutty flavor and is well worth its price. Although it is best known as the cheese to be grated over pasta, it is a superb dessert cheese. It is especially good when served with ripe pears and walnuts.

Semi-Hard Cheeses

◆ *Aged Sheep's Milk* Cheese: There is a variety of these delicious cheeses from all over the world to choose from. Amongst the best are Brebis Pyrénées from the French Basque region, the Caciottas from the Tuscan region of Italy, and Manchego from La Mancha in Spain. A truly outstanding domestic cheese in this category is Major Farm Mountain Shepherd from Vermont. These cheeses have a full, mellow flavor and are very good with pâté, *saucissons*, olives, and chilled white or rosé wine.

◆ *Emmenthaler:* The original golden Swiss cheese has a distinctively nutty flavor. It is excellent with apples, cherries, and plums.

◆ *Gruyère:* This heartier, nuttier Swiss is best known for its use in quiches and tarts. But it is also very good when served with thinly sliced sausage or salami. Comté, a French Gruyère, is a bit firmer and drier, and goes well with a mild sausage and a red Côtes-du-Rhone.

Soft-Ripened Cheeses

These cheeses have a variety of flavors and are wonderful to take on picnics, but they require careful handling. Bring only the amount of cheese you intend to serve because leftover soft-ripened cheeses are not good travellers. Try to buy a whole 8-ounce wheel of cheese rather than a wedge cut from a larger wheel. Look for cheese with a clean white rind. If the rind has lines, dark spots, or a brownish tinge, the cheese is probably overripe and no longer desirable.

◆ *Brie:* Brie is probably the most popular French cheese in this country. It has a smooth and buttery flavor. Brie de Meaux, which is more intense and fruity, is considered the best of the French Bries. To check for ripeness, the cheese should be supple, not stiff to the touch. Brie is delicious when served with crisp baguettes and chilled Mâcon-Villages. It is also excellent with juicy ripe peaches and strawberries.

◆ *Camembert:* This is a wonderful rich and creamy cheese. Good, buttery Camemberts include the popular Vallée or Royal brands from France. Le Châtelaine from Normandy and the superb Blythedale Farms from Vermont are more assertive and delicious. Be careful not to cut Camembert before it is fully ripened or it will never achieve its full potential.

Chèvres

These tangy goat's milk cheeses are very good for outdoor eating, especially with ripe tomatoes, olives, capers, and fruity olive oil. They are also delicious for dessert. Serve chèvres with berries, grapes, and peaches.

Some good basic chèvres are Montrachet and aged Boucheron from France and Caprini from Italy. Excellent domestic choices include Cypress Grove chèvres from California and Coach Farms from New York State.

Salads
and
Side Dishes

Red Cabbage, Pepper, and Onion Coleslaw with Orange-Cumin Vinaigrette

Serves 8 to 12

his is a spicy, subtly sweet coleslaw. It is a wonderful accompaniment to grilled chicken, fish, or a sandwich.

½ head red cabbage, thinly sliced
   (6 cups)
1 medium red bell pepper, seeded,
   deveined, and thinly sliced
1 medium yellow bell pepper, seeded,
   deveined, and thinly sliced
1 medium red onion, peeled,
   quartered, and thinly sliced
½ cup golden raisins
2 tablespoons red wine vinegar
4 tablespoons fresh orange juice
1 tablespoon fresh lime juice
⅓ cup mayonnaise
1 teaspoon ground cumin
½ cup extra-virgin olive oil
Salt and freshly ground black pepper,
   to taste

1. Put the cabbage, red pepper, yellow pepper, onion, and raisins in a very large bowl. Toss together until well combined.

2. In a medium bowl mix the vinegar, orange juice, and lime juice together. Gently stir in the mayonnaise and cumin until well combined. Whisk in the olive oil until the vinaigrette is creamy and thickened and all of the oil has been incorporated.

3. Pour the vinaigrette over the cabbage mixture and toss well. Add the salt and pepper to taste and mix well again. Cover the coleslaw and chill until ready to serve.

SUMMER TOMATOES WITH GORGONZOLA DRESSING

Serves 6 to 8

This robust combination of sweet, sun-ripened tomatoes and pungent dressing made with Gorgonzola, one of Italy's great cheeses, is a sure hit at a picnic. Serve with crusty baguettes or toasted garlic bread.

2 tablespoons red wine vinegar
6 tablespoons extra-virgin olive oil
Salt and freshly ground black pepper,
   to taste
½ pound Gorgonzola cheese,
   at room temperature
6 large ripe tomatoes
   (about 4 pounds), cored
   and thickly sliced

1. Combine the vinegar, olive oil, and salt and pepper in a mixing bowl and blend well with a whisk.

2. Add the cheese to the dressing and gently mash it with a fork. The dressing should be slightly lumpy.

3. Arrange the tomato slices in an overlapping pattern on a serving dish. Pour the dressing over the tomatoes and serve immediately.

Jicama, Orange, Watercress, and Pecan Salad

Serves 6

I like to use raw jicama in summer dishes because it retains its wonderful crunchy texture for a long time. This light and refreshing salad is ideal for hot weather picnics and it is very good when paired with Tarragon-Rosemary Roasted Chicken (page 56).

3 medium jicama (about 2½ pounds), peeled and cut into 2-inch-thick by 2½-inch-long strips

2 tablespoons fresh lime juice

3 medium oranges, peeled and cut into 1-inch pieces

1 medium red onion, peeled and thinly sliced

1 bunch watercress, rinsed and stemmed

½ cup chopped pecans

⅓ cup red wine vinegar

½ teaspoon ground cumin

Salt and freshly ground black pepper, to taste

½ cup extra-virgin olive oil

1 head Boston lettuce

1. Place the jicama strips in a large bowl. Add the lime juice and toss well. Add the orange pieces, onion, watercress, and pecans and toss again.

2. Stir the vinegar, cumin, and salt and pepper together in a medium bowl. Whisk in the olive oil until thickened. Taste and adjust the seasonings, if necessary. Pour over the jicama mixture, and toss. Taste and adjust the seasonings again if necessary, and gently toss again.

3. To serve, arrange the lettuce leaves in a shallow serving bowl. Spoon the jicama salad over the lettuce. Serve immediately.

New Potato, Green Bean, and Dill Salad

Serves 6

*P*otato salad is a perfect picnic food—it allows the cook to be inventive with a great variety of ingredients, depending on what's fresh and in season. This version, with fresh green beans, is particularly tasty. Be sure to mix the vinaigrette into the potatoes and beans while they are still warm.

---

3 pounds (about 12 medium) red
  new potatoes
1 pound fresh green beans, trimmed
  and cut into 2-inch pieces
1 teaspoon Dijon mustard
¼ cup red wine vinegar
⅓ cup extra-virgin olive oil
Salt and freshly ground black pepper
6 tablespoons chopped red onion
¼ cup chopped fresh dill

---

1. Put the potatoes in a steamer over a pot of boiling water and cook until tender, about 20 minutes. Drain and cool the potatoes, and then peel and quarter them and put them in a large bowl.

2. Put the beans into a medium pot of boiling salted water and simmer until crisp-tender, 3 to 5 minutes. Drain and cool the beans, and then add them to the bowl with the potatoes.

3. Whisk the mustard and vinegar together in a small bowl. Slowly add the olive oil, whisking constantly, until the vinaigrette thickens.

4. Toss the potatoes and green beans together. Add the salt and pepper, the red onion, and dill and toss again. Pour the vinaigrette over this mixture, toss carefully, and adjust the seasoning, if necessary.

5. Serve at room temperature.

MUSSEL AND POTATO SALAD

Serves 6

I love the unbeatable combination of mussels and potatoes. When eating in a French restaurant I will invariably order *moules* and *pommes frites*. This salad pairs mussels steamed in garlic, white wine, and herbs with boiled new potatoes and it is truly delicious. Since this salad contains both shellfish and mayonnaise, refrigerate it until ready to pack it, then put it in your cooler with ice or frozen gel packs and keep the cooler in the shade.

2 pounds (about 12 small), red new
   potatoes, scrubbed
1 tablespoon olive oil
3 cloves garlic, thinly sliced
1 cup dry white wine
1 tablespoon herbes de Provence
2 pounds mussels, well scrubbed
   and bearded
½ cup finely chopped red onion
½ cup finely chopped flat-leaf parsley
½ cup mayonnaise
1 tablespoon Dijon mustard
1 teaspoon white vinegar
Salt and freshly ground pepper,
   to taste

1. Put the potatoes in a a large pot of salted water. Bring to a boil, and boil gently, uncovered, until tender, about 20 to 25 minutes. Drain the potatoes and let cool.

2. Meanwhile, heat the olive oil in a large stockpot over medium heat. Add the garlic and sauté for 2 minutes. Add the wine and herbes de Provence, and bring to a boil. Add the mussels, lower the heat slightly, cover, and cook until mussels open, 4 to 6 minutes. Using a slotted spoon, remove the mussels to a bowl and reserve the cooking liquid. Discard any unopened mussels. Set aside to cool.

3. Strain the mussel cooking liquid through a wire-mesh sieve lined with cheesecloth into a small bowl and reserve.

4. Cut the potatoes into half-inch cubes and put them in a large bowl. Remove the mussels from their shells and add them to the bowl. Add the onions and ¼ cup of the parsley and stir to mix.

5. Put the mayonnaise into a medium bowl. Add ¼ cup of the reserved mussel cooking liquid, mustard, vinegar, and salt and pepper. Stir to blend well. Fold the mayonnaise mixture into the potato mixture and gently mix together. Taste and adjust the seasonings, if necessary.

6. Spoon the salad into a shallow bowl and top with the remaining chopped parsley. Refrigerate until ready to serve.

Summer Vegetables with Saffron Aioli

Serves 6 to 8

*A*ioli is a strong garlicky mayonnaise originating from the Provence region in southern France. Garden-fresh vegetables accompanied by aioli sauce make a wonderful presentation for a festive picnic. The colors are beautiful and the flavors are deliciously intense.

AIOLI SAUCE:

10 cloves garlic

2 large egg yolks, at room
   temperature (see Note)

Pinch of saffron threads

Salt and freshly ground white pepper,
   to taste

3 tablespoons fresh lemon juice

1 teaspoon Dijon mustard

¾ cup olive oil

½ cup peanut oil

VEGETABLES:

1 pound snow peas, trimmed,
   blanched, and refreshed in cold
   water

1 pound green beans, trimmed,
   blanched, and refreshed in cold
   water

1 pound carrots, peeled, cut into
   2-inch-long pieces, blanched,
   and refreshed in cold water

1 medium head cauliflower, cut into
   florets, blanched, and refreshed in
   cold water

3 medium red or green bell peppers,
   seeded, deveined, and sliced

1 pint cherry tomatoes, rinsed
   and stemmed

1 pound zucchini, sliced

1 pound small red new potatoes,
   steamed until tender, peeled,
   and halved

---

1. Purée the garlic in a blender or food processor fitted with a steel blade. Whisk the egg yolks in a small bowl until light in color and add to the garlic. Add the saffron, salt and pepper, lemon juice, and mustard and blend or process until smooth.

2. With the machine running, pour the oils very slowly into the mixture in a thin, steady stream, blending constantly. Continue blending until the sauce is thickened and firm. Transfer the aioli to a glass jar or bowl, cover with plastic wrap and refrigerate until ready to use. The aioli can be made up to a day ahead of time.

3. To serve, place the aioli in a bowl in the center of a large serving platter or basket. Arrange the prepared vegetables around it.

Note: The use of raw egg in a recipe can, in rare cases, cause salmonella poisoning. If this concerns you, the aioli sauce can be made with coddled eggs. To coddle the eggs, gently place 2 room-temperature eggs in a pan of boiling water. Turn off the heat, cover the pan, and let the eggs set for 1 minute. Remove immediately and shell. The yolks will be runny and the whites slightly coagulated.

GRILLED GARLIC SHRIMP,
WHITE BEAN, AND ARUGULA SALAD

Serves 6 to 8

*H*ere is a tasty and beautiful salad made with garlicky shrimp and complemented with savory white beans and arugula. Bring this to a potluck picnic dinner and watch it disappear.

1 cup white beans, picked over
   and rinsed
2 cups chicken stock, preferably
   homemade
2 cups water
1 medium yellow onion, peeled
2 small carrots, peeled and cut in
   half crosswise
¾ cup extra-virgin olive oil
2 cloves garlic, thinly sliced
1 tablespoon chopped fresh
   rosemary
2 tablespoons dry white wine
3 tablespoons balsamic vinegar
Salt and freshly ground pepper,
   to taste
1 pound large shrimp, peeled
   and deveined

2 tablespoons fresh lemon juice
1 bunch arugula, rinsed and
   stemmed

1. Put the beans in a medium bowl and add cold water to cover by about 2 inches. Soak for 6 to 8 hours or overnight. Change the water once or twice during soaking.

2. Drain the beans and put them in a stockpot. Add the chicken stock, water, onion, and carrots. Bring to a boil over high heat, then reduce the heat, cover, and simmer for 50 to 60 minutes, stirring occasionally, until just tender. Be careful not to overcook or boil the beans.

3. Drain and rinse the beans. Discard the onion and carrots. Place the beans in a large bowl.

4. Meanwhile, make the marinade for the shrimp. Put ¼ cup of the olive oil, the garlic, rosemary, wine, 1 table-spoon of the vinegar, and salt and pepper in a large glass or ceramic bowl and whisk together. Rinse the shrimp and pat them dry. Add the shrimp to the bowl and stir gently to coat with the marinade. Cover and refrigerate for 1 hour, stirring occa-sionally.

5. Preheat the broiler.

6. Remove the shrimp from the mari-nade, arrange them on an aluminum foil–lined broiler tray, and broil for about 5 minutes, until pink. Turn the shrimp once during cooking.

7. Add the shrimp to the beans, sprin-kle with the lemon juice, add the arugula, and toss together.

8. Mix the remaining 2 tablespoons of the vinegar and the remaining ½ cup olive oil together in a small bowl. Pour the mixture over the salad and toss. Taste and adjust the seasonings, if necessary and toss again.

9. Serve chilled or at room tempera-ture.

ORZO, SALMON, CORN, AND CHIVE SALAD

Serves 8

This irresistible salad is made with the unbeatable combination of orzo, poached salmon, fresh corn, and chives. I often make this with leftover grilled salmon and corn from the previous night's barbecue.

One 6-ounce salmon steak

1 teaspoon white vinegar

1 medium carrot, peeled and thinly sliced

1 rib celery, rinsed and halved crosswise

Salt and freshly ground pepper, to taste

1 pound orzo

2 tablespoons fresh lemon juice

1½ cups cooked fresh corn kernels (from 2 ears fresh corn)

½ cup minced chives

2 tablespoons balsamic vinegar

½ cup extra-virgin olive oil

1. To prepare the salmon, place the salmon steak in a shallow saucepan and cover with cold water. Add the vinegar, carrot, celery, and salt and pepper to the pan. Bring to a boil, lower the heat and simmer, uncovered, for about 3 minutes for a pink center. Poach a bit longer, up to 2 minutes, if desired. Do not overcook. Remove the salmon from the poaching liquid, drain and set aside to cool.

2. Meanwhile, bring a large pot of salted water to a boil and cook the orzo until al dente, 10 to 12 minutes. Drain well.

3. Put the orzo in a large bowl, drizzle the lemon juice over it, and toss well. Add the corn and chives to the orzo and toss again.

4. Using a fork, remove the salmon from the bone and gently break the meat apart with your fingers. Add the salmon pieces to the orzo mixture and gently toss again.

5. Add the balsamic vinegar, olive oil, and additional salt and pepper and toss until well combined. Taste and adjust the seasonings, if necessary.

6. Serve cold or at room temperature. You may want to refresh the salad with a dash of lemon and olive oil just before serving.

Lemon-Pecan Chicken Salad

Serves 6

*C*hicken salad, the mainstay of summer picnics, can be made in so many ways. It can be simply tossed with a bit of mayonnaise, herbs, and any number of chopped vegetables or fruit. This lemony chicken salad is especially good served on leaves of chilled endive and radicchio.

---

1 medium yellow onion, peeled

2 medium carrots, peeled

2 stalks celery, trimmed and halved, plus 1 cup diced celery

12 parsley sprigs

12 whole black peppercorns

4 whole cloves

Salt, to taste

3 whole boneless, skinless chicken breasts

1 cup mayonnaise

1 tablespoon Dijon mustard

1 tablespoon fresh lemon juice

1 cup chopped pecans

1 cup watercress, rinsed, stemmed, and dried

Salt and freshly ground pepper, to taste

---

1. Put the onion, carrots, celery stalks, and parsley in a large stockpot. Add 4 quarts of water to cover, then add the peppercorns, cloves, and salt. Bring to a boil, then reduce the heat, and simmer, uncovered, for 15 minutes.

2. Add the chicken breasts to the simmering broth, raise the heat, and return to a boil, then reduce the heat and gently simmer for 25 minutes. Remove the pot from the heat and let the chicken cool in the broth.

3. When the chicken is cool enough to handle, remove it from the broth. Strain the broth and reserve for another use. Tear the meat into bite-sized pieces and place the pieces in a large bowl.

4. Mix the mayonnaise, mustard, and lemon juice together in a medium bowl. Add the mixture to the chicken and gently toss together until well mixed. Add the pecans, the diced celery, and the watercress and toss again until well mixed. Season with salt and pepper. Cover and refrigerate for 1 hour before serving.

5. Served chilled.

` ` ` ` ` ` ` ` ` ` ` ` `

A Lakeside Salad Supper

◆

*Herbed Green Beans with
Mozzarella and Prosciutto*

◆

*Grilled Garlic Shrimp, White Bean,
and Arugula Salad*

Lemon-Pecan Chicken Salad

*Summer Tomatoes
with Gorgonzola Dressing*

◆

assorted breads

◆

Cinnamon-Peach Cake

◆

*champagne
sparkling water*

GRILLED MEXICAN CHICKEN SALAD

Serves 6 to 8

*T*his spicy chicken salad, made with corn, avocados and chile peppers, is rich in color, taste, and texture. It is delicious served with cornbread and dark Mexican beer.

---

3 whole chicken breasts (about 3
   pounds), split
Juice of 3 medium lemons
   (½ cup juice)
Juice of 3 limes (½ cup plus
   2 tablespoons juice)
4 cloves garlic, thinly sliced
1 tablespoon cumin seed
1¼ cups olive oil
1 pint cherry tomatoes, halved
1½ cups cooked fresh corn kernels
   (from 2 ears sweet corn)
½ cup chopped scallions
1 teaspoon finely minced fresh
   green chile pepper
2 ripe avocados
3 tablespoons chopped fresh cilantro
Salt and freshly ground black pepper,
   to taste

---

1. Place the chicken in a large glass or ceramic baking dish. Combine the lemon juice, ½ cup of the lime juice, the garlic, and cumin seed in a medium bowl. Slowly whisk in ¾ cup of the oil. Pour the marinade over the chicken. Cover and refrigerate overnight, turning occasionally.

2. Prepare a charcoal or gas grill or preheat the broiler.

3. Remove the chicken from the marinade and grill or broil about 6 to 8 inches from the heat for 10 to 15 minutes on each side until nicely browned and the juices run clear when the chicken is pricked with a fork. Baste often with the marinade during grilling.

4. Remove the chicken from the grill and set aside to cool slightly. When the chicken is cool enough to handle, remove the meat from the bones and tear it into pieces about 1½ inches long.

5. Place the meat in a large bowl. Add the tomatoes, corn, scallions, and chile pepper to the chicken and set aside.

6. Peel, pit, and dice the avocado. Reserve 2 tablespoons of the avocado and put the remaining avocado in a small bowl.

7. To prepare the dressing, mash the reserved 2 tablespoons avocado in a small bowl and beat in the remaining 2 tablespoons lime juice with a fork until blended. Whisk in the remaining ¼ cup oil until well blended. Pour the mixture over the diced avocado and toss together. Pour the dressing over the chicken salad.

8. Add the cilantro and salt and pepper and toss. Taste and adjust the seasoning, if necessary.

9. Serve at room temperature.

Main Dishes

GRILLED CHICKEN KEBABS
WITH PEACH SALSA

Serves 6 (makes 1½ cups salsa)

These grilled chicken kebabs are a tasty main course served with tangy peach salsa on the side. The salsa is very versatile—it is an excellent accompaniment to barbecued beef or pork, or it can be served as a dip with vegetables or chips, and it can be made up to three days in advance. This a a great dish for a late-afternoon beach barbecue.

CHICKEN:

¾ cup olive oil

¼ cup fresh lemon juice

8 cloves garlic, halved

1 tablespoon herbes de Provence

Salt and freshly ground black pepper, to taste

3 whole boneless, skinless chicken breasts, rinsed and patted dry, and cut into 1½-inch cubes

PEACH SALSA:

1 tablespoon olive oil

12 cloves garlic, thinly sliced

8 shallots, peeled and thinly sliced

1 cup dry white wine

4 large peaches, peeled, pitted, and cut into ½-inch-thick wedges

2 plum tomatoes, cut into ½-inch-thick wedges

1 tablespoon low-sodium soy sauce

½ cup dark brown sugar

½ teaspoon red-pepper flakes

1. To prepare the chicken: Combine the olive oil, lemon juice, garlic, herbes de Provence, and salt and pepper in a large glass or ceramic bowl. Add the chicken pieces, toss well, cover, and refrigerate for 6 to 8 hours to marinate.

2. To prepare the salsa: Heat the olive oil in a large sauté pan over medium heat. Add the garlic and shallots and cook for about 10 minutes, until softened and golden. Add the wine, bring to a boil, and then reduce the heat and simmer, uncovered, for 15 minutes. Add the peaches, tomatoes, soy sauce, brown sugar, and red pepper flakes to the pan and bring to a boil over high heat. Reduce the heat to medium and cook for 20 minutes, stirring frequently. The peaches and tomatoes should be broken down but remain fairly chunky. Taste and adjust the seasonings, if necessary. Remove from the heat, let cool, and refrigerate until ready to serve. *Note: the salsa can be made up to 3 days ahead of time at this point.*

3. Prepare a gas or charcoal grill to medium-hot.

4. To make the kebabs: Thread 6 skewers with the marinated chicken squares. Grill the kebabs 5 or 6 inches from the coals for about 10 to 12 minutes, turning them occasionally, until the chicken is cooked through.

5. Serve the kebabs immediately with a few spoonfuls of peach salsa on the side.

Tarragon-Rosemary
Roasted Chicken

Serves 8

*W*hat could be better sometimes than a simple roasted chicken? This is essential picnic food. The chicken is delicious on its own or with any number of side dishes and salads.

---

2 whole chickens, about 4 pounds each, rinsed and patted dry

1 medium yellow onion, peeled and cut into large chunks

1 medium lemon, quartered

4 sprigs tarragon

2 sprigs rosemary

1 tablespoon unsalted butter, at room temperature

Salt and freshly ground black pepper, to taste

---

1. Preheat the oven to 425°F.

2. Place the chickens on a rack in a large roasting pan. Stuff the cavities with the onion, lemon, tarragon, and rosemary. Truss with kitchen string. Rub the butter all over the skin of both chickens and season generously with salt and pepper.

3. Roast the chickens for 15 minutes. Reduce the oven temperature to 375°F and continue roasting until the juices run clear when the thigh is pierced with a fork, about 1 hour and 20 minutes. Remove from the oven and let cool slightly, about 10 minutes, before carving.

4. Serve the chicken warm or at room temperature, or refrigerate the chicken before carving and serve cold.

FUSILLI WITH FRESH MOZZARELLA, TOMATOES, AND OLIVES

Serves 6 to 8

*T*his is a quick and easy pasta dish to make for an impromptu picnic on a hot summer day. Use the best ingredients you can find—fresh mozzarella, vine-ripened tomatoes, and fresh aromatic basil.

½ pound fresh mozzarella,
  cut into ¼-inch cubes
4 large ripe tomatoes (about 3
  pounds), cut into ½-inch dice
½ cup (about 3 ounces) black olives,
  pitted and coarsely chopped
3 cloves garlic, minced
6 tablespoons coarsely chopped
  fresh basil
¼ cup finely chopped flat-leaf parsley
½ cup extra-virgin olive oil
Salt and freshly ground black pepper,
  to taste
1½ pounds fusilli

---

1. Combine the mozzarella, tomatoes, olives, garlic, basil, parsley, olive oil, and salt and pepper together in a large bowl. Set aside.

2. Meanwhile bring a large pot of salted water to a boil. Cook the pasta until al dente, about 10 minutes. Drain well.

3. Add the pasta to the mozzarella and tomato mixture and toss well. Taste and adjust the seasonings, if necessary.

4. Serve chilled or at room temperature.

POACHED SALMON WITH BASIL VINAIGRETTE

Serves 6

This is a lovely, elegant recipe of lightly poached salmon topped with a fresh basil vinaigrette. I highly recommend adding this versatile sauce to your cooking repertoire. I like to add it to chicken, fish, and cold pasta dishes, and it is remarkable drizzled over fresh, ripe tomatoes.

POACHED SALMON:

6 boneless salmon steaks (about 6
    ounces each)
3 tablespoons white vinegar
1 cup thinly sliced yellow onions
½ cup thinly sliced carrots
6 parsley sprigs
1 teaspoon dried thyme
3 whole cloves
6 whole peppercorns
Salt to taste

BASIL VINAIGRETTE:

2 teaspoons Dijon mustard
2 tablespoons capers, drained
2 tablespoons chopped fresh parsley
2 tablespoons chopped fresh basil
1 tablespoon white vinegar
1 tablespoon fresh lemon juice
Salt and freshly ground black pepper,
    to taste
½ cup corn or canola oil
½ cup olive oil

1. To prepare the salmon: Place the salmon steaks in a large, shallow saucepan and cover with cold water. Add the remaining ingredients to the pan. Bring to a boil, and then lower the heat and simmer, uncovered, for about 3 minutes for a pink center. Poach a bit longer if desired. Do not overcook. Remove the steaks from the poaching liquid with a slotted spoon and drain. Set aside, or refrigerate if serving the salmon cold.

2. To prepare the vinaigrette: Place all of the ingredients except the corn and olive oils in the bowl of a food processor fitted with a steel blade. Pulse 4 or 5 times. With the machine running, add the oils in a thin stream until they are well incorporated. Taste and correct seasoning, if necessary.

3. Serve the salmon cold or at room temperature topped with 2 or 3 spoonfuls of the vinaigrette.

ROASTED FILLET OF BEEF AND RED
AND YELLOW PEPPERS WITH CAPER VINAIGRETTE

Serves 6 to 8

*H*ere is a stunning dish of fillet of beef, with its wonderful, rich flavor, and colorful red and yellow peppers drizzled with caper vinaigrette. The roasted peppers and the vinaigrette can be made a few hours before roasting the beef, and the dish can be assembled just before serving.

ROASTED PEPPERS:

3 medium red bell peppers, seeded, deveined, and halved

3 medium yellow bell peppers, seeded, deveined, and halved

3 tablespoons olive oil

FILLET OF BEEF:

One 4- to 5-pound beef fillet, trimmed and tied

2 cloves garlic, halved lengthwise

1 tablespoon kosher salt

Freshly ground black pepper, to taste

VINAIGRETTE:

1 tablespoon Dijon mustard

2 tablespoons balsamic vinegar

2 tablespoons capers, drained

Salt and freshly ground pepper, to taste

½ cup extra-virgin olive oil

---

1. To prepare the peppers, preheat the oven to 375°F. Place the pepper halves in an aluminum foil–lined roasting pan and pour 2 tablespoons of the olive oil over them. Roast the peppers, turning them once or twice, until they are softened and lightly browned, 50 minutes to 1 hour. Remove the peppers from the oven and set aside.

2. To prepare the beef: Preheat the oven to 450°F. Rub the meat with the garlic, brush it with the remaining 1

tablespoon olive oil, sprinkle it with the salt, and season generously with the pepper. Place the meat on a roasting rack set in a shallow roasting pan. Roast for 10 minutes and then reduce the heat to 350°F. For rare, roast for 25 minutes longer, or until a meat thermometer registers 120°F; for medium, roast for 35 minutes longer or until a meat thermometer registers 130°F.

3. Remove the fillet from the oven and let it stand for about 10 minutes to give the juices time to collect before carving it into ¾-inch-thick slices.

4. To prepare the vinaigrette: Place the mustard in a small bowl, add the vinegar, capers, and salt and pepper and whisk well. Slowly drizzle in the olive oil, whisking constantly until the vinaigrette is thickened.

5. To serve, arrange the beef slices on a platter slightly overlapping and alternating with the peppers. Serve immediately with the caper vinaigrette on the side.

Safety

*Y*ou can't be too careful when handling and packing food for cooking and eating outdoors. Since summer heat increases the chance of bacterial growth in foods, and bacteria are more likely to grow in foods that are high in protein and moisture—meats, poultry, seafood, dairy products, and egg dishes—the basics of food safety bear repeating.

◆ Wash your hands thoroughly before and after handling food. Clean your cutting surfaces and utensils with hot, soapy water after each use.

◆ Refrigerate all foods prepared ahead of time. Pack them in a cooler surrounded by ice or frozen gel packs to keep the food under 40°F. For picnics away from home, take only the amount of food you'll need.

◆ Thaw and marinate meats, poultry, and seafood in the refrigerator—not at room temperature.

◆ Cook meat, poultry, and seafood thoroughly. Don't start to cook, then stop, intending to finish later; bacteria grow faster in partially cooked food.

◆ Eat hot, grilled foods immediately and serve on clean plates.

◆ Refrigerate perishable foods, including leftovers, within 2 hours. Food left in a cooler should be safe to eat if the cooler still has ice in it and if the food is cool to your touch.

Biscuits, Cookies, and Desserts

COUNTRY-STYLE BUTTERMILK BISCUITS

Makes 16 biscuits

*T*ry this old-fashioned biscuit recipe for a picnic with Southern flair. The biscuits are wonderful served Virginia-style—spread with sweet butter and paper-thin slices of honey-baked ham—or as an accompaniment to Chilled Carrot, Orange, and Chive Soup (page 21).

2 cups unbleached all-purpose flour
1 tablespoon baking powder
1 teaspoon sugar
¼ teaspoon baking soda
½ teaspoon salt
Freshly ground black pepper, to taste
5 tablespoons vegetable shortening
¾ cup buttermilk
4 tablespoons melted butter

1. Preheat the oven to 425°F.

2. Combine the flour, baking powder, sugar, baking soda, salt, and pepper in a large mixing bowl. Using a pastry blender or your fingertips, cut the shortening into the mixture until it resembles coarse meal. Add the buttermilk and gently stir until the mixture forms a mass. Using your hands, gather the dough into a ball.

3. Transfer the dough to a lightly floured work surface and knead for about 1 minute. Pat or roll the dough out to form a rectangle ¾-inch thick. Using a 2-inch biscuit cutter, cut out about 16 biscuits. Use up all of the dough.

4. Place the biscuits about 1 inch apart on a baking sheet. Brush the tops of the biscuits with the melted butter. Bake until golden, 10 to 12 minutes. Remove biscuits from the oven and transfer to a wire rack to cool.

LEMON WAFERS

Makes 2 dozen cookies

These crisp cookies are delicious with ice cream or sorbet; they're also perfect for dipping into iced espresso. They keep beautifully in an airtight container until ready to serve.

---

6 tablespoons unsalted butter,
  at room temperature
1 cup granulated sugar
1 egg, at room temperature
1¼ cups unbleached all-purpose
  flour
4 ounces almonds, ground
1½ tablespoons fresh lemon juice

---

1. Preheat the oven to 350°F. Lightly butter 2 baking sheets.

2. In a large bowl, mix together the butter, sugar, and egg with an electric mixer on medium speed until smooth.

3. Stir in the flour, almonds, and lemon juice and mix until well combined.

4. Spoon the dough onto the baking sheets then press the dough into 2½-inch rounds with floured fingers.

5. Place the baking sheets on the middle rack of the oven and bake for 10 to 12 minutes, until the edges are lightly browned. Remove the cookies with a spatula and cool on racks.

6. Store the cookies in an airtight container until ready to serve.

Cinnamon-Peach Cake

Serves 6 to 8

This cake takes advantage of midsummer peaches when they are at their peak. No plates or forks are necessary since it is simply cut into squares and eaten out of hand.

Butter and flour, for baking pan
1 cup unbleached all-purpose flour
1 teaspoon baking powder
½ cup (1 stick) unsalted butter, softened
½ cup firmly packed light brown sugar
½ cup plus 3 tablespoons granulated sugar
2 large eggs, at room temperature
2½ cups ripe peaches (about 3 peaches), peeled and thinly sliced
½ teaspoon ground cinnamon

---

1. Preheat the oven to 350°F. Lightly butter and flour an 8-inch square baking pan.

2. In a medium bowl, whisk together the flour and baking powder.

3. In a large bowl, using an electric mixer on high speed, cream the butter, brown sugar, and ½ cup of the granulated sugar for about 3 minutes, until light and fluffy.

4. With the mixer running on medium speed, add the flour mixture to the batter a little at a time; do not overmix. Beat in the eggs.

5. Scrape the batter into the prepared pan. Smooth the surface and then arrange the sliced peaches on top of the batter.

6. In a small bowl, combine the remaining 3 tablespoons sugar with the cinnamon and sprinkle the mixture over the peaches.

7. Bake for about 1 hour, or until the cake begins to pull away from the sides of the pan and turns golden brown.

8. Remove the cake from the oven and cool in the pan on a wire rack. When completely cool, serve the cake directly from the pan or remove it from the pan, cut it into squares, and serve it fruit-side up.

PERFECT PICNIC BROWNIES

Serves 6 to 8 (makes 16 brownies)

$\mathcal{B}$rownies seem to be everyone's favorite dessert, and this recipe is sure to please. These brownies depend on the use of high-quality ingredients. Use the best chocolate available, and the freshest butter and eggs.

Butter and flour, for the baking pan
5 ounces unsweetened chocolate,
  preferably Callebaut or Valrhona
½ cup (1 stick) unsalted butter,
  at room temperature
1¼ cups sugar
½ teaspoon vanilla extract
3 large eggs, at room temperature
¾ cup unbleached all-purpose flour
½ cup walnuts, chopped
Confectioners' sugar, sifted

---

1. Preheat the oven to 325°F. Butter and flour an 8-inch square baking pan.

2. Melt the chocolate and butter on the top of a double boiler. Remove from the heat and let cool for 5 minutes.

3. Put the sugar in a medium bowl and stir in the chocolate mixture. Mix with an electric mixer on medium speed until well blended and smooth, about 30 seconds. Scrape down the inside of the bowl with a rubber spatula.

4. Add the vanilla to the chocolate mixture. Add the eggs one at a time with the mixer on low speed. After the eggs are well incorporated, scrape the bowl and blend again until the mixture is very smooth, about 20 seconds.

5. Add the flour to the chocolate mixture and mix well by hand. Stir in the walnuts.

6. Spread the batter evenly in the prepared pan. Place on the center oven rack and bake just until a thin crust forms on the top, about 35 minutes. A knife inserted in the center should come out clean.

7. Remove the pan from the oven and cool on a wire rack for 1 hour.

8. To serve, sift a bit of confectioners' sugar over the top and cut into squares.

` ` ` ` ` ` ` ` ` ` ` `

A Late-Afternoon Beach Barbecue

◆

*Spicy Black Bean Dip
with Tortilla Chips*

◆

*Grilled Chicken Kebabs
with Peach Salsa*

*Orzo, Salmon, Corn,
and Chive Salad*

mixed green salad

◆

Perfect Picnic Brownies

◆

*Mexican beer
chilled white wine
sparkling cider*

CHILLED MINTED FRUIT

Serves 6

This is one of my favorite ways to serve fruit on a hot day. You can use any combination of fresh fruits, but I especially like using cherries, blueberries, and red grapes. A beautiful and refreshing picnic finale.

12 ice cubes
1 pound ripe cherries, rinsed
1 cup blueberries, rinsed
1 cup red grapes, rinsed
¾ cup thinly sliced mint leaves

1. Crush the ice in a blender by filling the cannister about three-quarters full of ice cubes. Turn the blender on high and grind up the ice. This may have to be done in two batches.

2. Fill a large bowl with the crushed ice, cherries, blueberries, grapes, and mint. Toss together. Refrigerate for at least 1 hour and serve chilled.

Index

TABLE OF EQUIVALENTS

The exact equivalents in the following tables have been rounded for convenience.

Liquid and Dry Measures

U.S.	Metric
¼ teaspoon	1.25 milliliters
½ teaspoon	2.5 milliliters
1 teaspoon	5 milliliters
1 tablespoon (3 teaspoons)	15 milliliters
1 fluid ounce (2 tablespoons)	30 milliliters
¼ cup	60 milliliters
⅓ cup	80 milliliters
1 cup	240 milliliters
1 pint (2 cups)	480 milliliters
1 quart (4 cups, 32 ounces)	960 milliliters
1 gallon (4 quarts)	3.84 liters
1 ounce (by weight)	28 grams
1 pound	454 grams
2.2 pounds	1 kilogram

Length Measures

U.S.	Metric
⅛ inch	3 millimeters
¼ inch	6 millimeters
½ inch	12 millimeters
1 inch	2.5 centimeters

Oven Temperatures

Fahrenheit	Celsius	Gas
250	120	½
275	140	1
300	150	2
325	160	3
350	180	4
375	190	5
400	200	6
425	220	7
450	230	8
475	240	9
500	260	10